THE MYSTERIOUS MR ISAAC

RICK BROWN

852
PRESS

What if the secret to success was sitting
right beside you on the train?

Also By Rick Brown

A Story for Another Time

The Three Boys

Falina

The Golden Gumnut

Chinese Whispers

THE MYSTERIOUS MR ISAAC

RICK BROWN

www.852Press.com.au

10 9 8 7 6 5 4 3 2 1

National Library of Australia Cataloguing-in-Publication entry:

Author: Brown, Rick (1954-)

Title: The Mysterious Mr Isacc / by Rick Brown

ISBN: 978-1-7641505-0-7 (paperback)

ISBN: 978-1-7641505-1-4 (ebook)

Australian fiction.

Cover Design: 852 Press

Dedication

This book would not have been possible without the dedicated staff and management of SureBridge, whose commitment to client service over nearly three decades helped bring our vision to life.

I would like to extend my sincere appreciation to Stephen Eager, whose dedication and support ensured our standards of service, policies, and procedures were consistently exemplary. My thanks go to him and his wife, Jenny, for their invaluable contributions.

Finally, I wish to acknowledge the two most important people in my life. My wife, Glenda, who not only skilfully guided SureBridge to success but also remained steadfast in her support for both me and the team. And our daughter, Jessica, who continues to make us proud through her own professional achievements, demonstrating the same passion and commitment to client service that has defined our journey.

Characters

Simon – Main character
Isaac – Asian man on the train
Judy – Simon's wife
Michael – Supplier boss
Old Boss – Simon's old boss
Christian – Old boss' wife's younger brother
Phillip – Old boss' oldest son
Jenny – Coffee shop owner
Mrs Miller – Owner of the business Judy worked at

Glossary

CFO – Chief Financial Officer
CRM – Customer Relationship Management software
MD – Managing Director
PA – Personal Assistant

Chapter One

Simon sat in the carriage along with the other thirty or so passengers. He could not hear a word over the silence of the still train. It sat at the station; the soft hum of the electric motor was the only sound flooding the space.

'Do people ever talk anymore?' he thought, looking out the window at the masses disappearing into the earth through the arches on the wall of the station. He looked back into the carriage. The number of people left was just enough to use every seat except the one next to him. No one stood in the aisles or near the doors. The majority just sat looking at their small, bright screens. Simon guessed many of them were talking with their fingers, perhaps to a family member, a friend, or their lover or partner. Maybe a virtual friend, someone they had never met but spoke to

via the digital world each morning or evening, as they made their way to and from work.

Some were smiling, but most just had that look of: my life sucks, shoot me now, or please get me off this bloody train.

Simon was none of these.

He was dissatisfied with his job; however, his domestic life in a small village near London was satisfactory. His wife, Judy, also found her work at a local trucking company, unfulfilling. The small cottage they purchased with the inheritance from his late father's estate allowed them to own the property and land outright. Therefore, money was not an issue as far as having to pay ridiculous sums of interest on a mortgage. They did, however, still have a small debt owing on a loan for the small car and furniture for the house. In all, life at home was good.

At that moment, the train lurched forward. Some people looked up, but most just stayed their course and remained locked in their digital void. Simon had about an hour to go before he arrived at his station. He wasn't a fan of the phone thing. A tool to call people or have people call him and send and receive messages was about the extent of his usage. He was a daydreamer, and, as usual, his mind was moving like a kaleidoscope as the train exploded from the underground into the bright sunlight of the English late summer evening.

He often thought about success and how to achieve it. His job as a computer industry salesman provided a reasonable income, but he knew there were higher-paying jobs that he figured might increase his happiness.

Simon had finished his schooling life in the middle of the scholastic percentile. His parents had never really pushed him to study, as very early in his school life they had succumbed to the clear fact that he was no genius and pushing him only made his grades worse. He did, however, spend much of his time after school involved in some form of sport. He had chosen rowing as his favourite. He loved staying fit and believed this sport exemplified perseverance and discipline. Each of the crew's effort for every stroke was visible through the puddles left by the oars pushing their way through the water. Slacking off for just one stroke during a race was not on, and Simon enjoyed it thoroughly.

After school, he realised university wasn't for him, so he found a retail job and excelled in sales. For several years, he honed his skills and accepted management training encouraged by his employers. He had continued his career in sales, transitioning from one product and company to another. In each instance, he achieved success; however, he had not yet found his true niche. It was only when he decided to purchase a computer while working at a chemical company that he discovered his passion. Subsequently, he began selling computers. Despite this progress, he still felt that something was missing.

The train stopped, and a few more people got off, but

only one got on. He was a small, frail man. He was clearly of Asian descent and appeared to have had a tough life. His grey, wispy hair sat straight, flowing gently over his pale skin. His suit looked old and about two sizes too big, as if he had put it on many years ago and shrunk inside it. His round wire-framed glasses sat atop his tiny nose, and behind them were two dark yet bright and alert eyes. The man moved gently down the aisle towards Simon and came up beside the empty seat next to him.

"Do you mind?" he asked in a soft but clear voice.

Simon said nothing, as he felt nothing needed to be said. After all, he just assumed it was a rhetorical question, and his sitting up straight and moving himself closer to the window was answer enough.

The small man sat and placed the newspaper he had been carrying under his arm onto his lap. He then reached into his coat pocket, the one next to Simon, and pulled out a deck of cards. For a few seconds, he moved the cards around and then looked up at Simon.

"You play?" he asked.

Chapter Two

Simon looked around, wondering if the man was asking someone else. Then, he looked down at the deck of cards, then back at the man.

"Who, me?" he asked, turning his shoulders to align with his head. "No, yes, I play, but no, I am ok for the moment; thanks anyway."

"You should, you know. It's a fantastic way to relax and take your mind off things," the man said, gently pushing the cards back into his pocket. "You know," the small man continued, "I have been travelling on these trains for the past thirty years. Each time I boarded the same carriage, I have consistently sat next to the same individual until their circumstances changed, rendering my presence on the train, for them, no longer necessary."

Simon was half-listening and was unsure whether he should respond or even if he wanted to. Seconds passed, and then minutes. Simon was looking out the window, but then he looked back to see if the man had started reading his paper or was looking elsewhere. No, he was still looking up at Simon, a gentle smile on his face. More time passed, and Simon, who had returned his view out the train window, looked back once again. The man was still there, still looking.

Finally, Simon asked. "Why?"

The man took a moment, then asked, "Why what?" the expression returning.

"Why do you do that? Get on and sit next to the same person?"

"Because they needed me."

Simon turned back to the window, but his daydreaming mind was gone and replaced with one full of questions.

He turned back. "Why do they need you?"

"Because they are lost," the man replied.

"On the train? They're lost?" Simon asked, as more questions flooded his head.

"No," the man replied and turned a little more toward Simon.

There was a pause for a short while as Simon waited for this strange man to elaborate on the previous answer. There was no response. Not getting any reply, just a smiling face, Simon asked, "Then how are they lost?"

With this, the man turned in his seat as the train slowed into the next station. He looked at Simon and then stood. His height now was just ever so slightly higher than Simon's, still sitting at the window.

"An answer for tomorrow," he replied as he turned and walked out and off the train.

Simon sat bewildered, unsure of what had just happened.

'*Who the hell was that?*' he thought, turning and moving to the seat the man had just left. Then, looking across the carriage so he could see out the opposite window, he watched the several people walking toward the exit, further along the small regional station's platform.

The train began to move, and then as it passed them, gathering speed, Simon studied the tiny crowd. There was no old Asian man within the group. He looked back toward the other end of the platform as it disappeared into the distance and saw no one. He sat back in his seat and surveyed the now empty carriage.

His station arrived just two stops later, and he disembarked. His mind was in a state of confusion. He speculated to himself, "Perhaps I fell asleep and was dreaming," speaking softly to no one in particular. As he proceeded past the unoccupied guard's room, he mused further, "Maybe my daydreaming has reached an entirely new level." Subsequently, he walked to his vehicle and drove home, a journey that took seven minutes.

Chapter Three
____

The following afternoon, Simon headed along King Street to Hammersmith Station. His mind was once again back on the train he had been on the day before. He had said nothing to Judy about the incident. In fact, he had told no one. He was thinking about each moment of the short meeting.

Was it real? Was it as he had felt the day before, just a dream?

He headed down to the Piccadilly line platform and waited with the other workers, shoppers, students, and various other people, all standing patiently for the train to Cockfosters. As it arrived, the crowd started to come alive, with people moving to the point where they knew from countless trips that a seat could be available. Simon, on the other hand, knew that his chosen carriage would be packed and then at Gloucester Road, many of the people in the carriage would get off, and a seat would become available before the carriage refilled with the oncoming passengers. As was almost always the case, this is what happened, and Simon got a seat next to the window on the right-hand side facing forward.

A young backpacker jumped in next to him a moment later and wrestled his huge pack onto his lap. "Sorry for the squeeze, mate," he said with a clearly Australian accent. "I'm only going to Green Park."

Simon settled back and relaxed.

The train rattled through to Green Park, and as promised, the young man stood and moved off with several other people out and off the train. Simon noticed as the train started off that the seat next to him was, in fact, empty. Clearly, yesterday was a daydream, and there was no old man. He couldn't remember precisely when the man had sat down next to him, but he did recall it was later in the trip. As they pulled out of Holborn, he again sat alone. At least he had not sensed anyone sitting next to him as he stared into the black window of the tube.

"Because they are not sure what to do next," a soft voice said from beside Simon.

"Shit!" Simon exclaimed as he turned to see the same old man again sitting looking up at him, the same soft smile on his face.

"So, you are for real, not a dream. Who are you, and

what do you want?" Simon all but whispered as he looked around, checking no one heard his words.

Clearly, no one did as many were transfixed, looking at their silver-lit screens, while others did as Simon had previously done, just staring at the inky black wall of the tunnel.

"Excellent questions, so let me answer them in order," he replied. "Firstly, yes, I am real and not a dream, although of the hundreds of people I have helped over the years, you are the first who thought I was a dream. Second, I am here to help you."

"I don't need help, or at least I'm not sure I do," Simon said, starting to relax just a little as he tried to understand what was happening.

"No one ever does," the man replied, then seeing the quizzical look start to appear on Simon's face, he added, "Think they need help."

"But what help do I need?" Simon asked again.

"Before I answer that, let me explain a few things. My name is Isaac. I know, a funny name for an Asian person, but it is Isaac, nonetheless. I have been helping people like you for many years. More than you could ever imagine." Isaac shuffled a little in his seat to face more towards Simon. "As for helping you, let me try explaining with a little story."

Simon was intrigued, unbelievably, so he listened. As the man started to speak, the train and the noise it created, both human and mechanical, seemed to fade to near silence.

"I once met a man," Isaac started, "who worked in a sporting goods business. He had been there for about five years and spent the best part of ten hours a day working with customers, moving stock, cleaning, and generally running the business."

"Meanwhile, his boss, the shop owner, spent much of his day in his office, sitting in front of his computer, and then at four each day, he would head off. No goodbyes, no job well done or pat on the back. He just left, leaving the business to be closed each afternoon by the man."

"Finally, a day came when a customer phoned and requested a particular product he needed to purchase. The man, our friend in the story, took notes and then advised the man that he would call him back as soon as he found what the customer requested, as he knew he didn't stock the requested item."

"After an exhaustive search across all his suppliers and worldwide by way of the internet, he couldn't find the product. As promised, he contacted the man and apologised that what the man wanted was not available anywhere."

"'Please check again, as I am sure it is available somewhere. I've seen it,' the man on the other end of the phone said. The shop assistant asked if the man could provide a brand or serial number that might help identify the item. The customer became abusive and told the assistant to just go find the product."

"Our friend apologised again and asked the customer to calm down. The customer then went off his head and abused the assistant, calling him incompetent and useless, then started to shout that what he wanted was, in fact, available as he had seen it on TV the night before."

"The assistant asked several more questions, only to discover that what the man had seen was, in fact, a product in a science fiction movie. Having deduced this, he was about to explain this very fact when the customer just hung up, yelling that he was going to call the man's boss. Our friend looked around to his boss's office only to see it empty. So, he figured that the customer would need to wait till the following day to speak to him."

"That afternoon, as the assistant was cleaning up and about to lock up, his personal phone rang. Not wanting to get caught on the security camera talking on his mobile in the office, he took it out of his pocket and was about to dismiss the call when he noticed it was his boss."

"Figuring that since it was the boss, he could answer the call, so he did. His boss explained that no one working for him should ever speak to a customer as he had done, nor should they ever disagree that a product is not available. He should have made a much bigger effort to discover where he could obtain it, or, at the very least, offer an alternative."

"The man was about to explain that there was no

product or any viable alternative when his boss told him that when he left and locked the door behind him, not to return. He was fired." Isaac paused his story, looking across at Simon to make sure he was still listening.

Simon was about to speak; however, Isaac raised his hand gently and then continued. He started explaining that their friend had always wanted to start his own business but lacked the confidence to do so. He doubted his ability to generate enough income quickly to cover expenses and provide for his basic needs, all which resulted in fear.

Isaac continued, "That afternoon, he closed the door, turned right and walked one mile to a local large sporting goods wholesaler and knocked on the door. The owner of the wholesale business, who knew him well, answered the door. Our friend, standing at the bottom of the two stairs down from where the owner stood, asked if they frequently received small orders that seemed insignificant and were not wholesale purchases. The owner confirmed that such orders were common and motioned that our friend should come in out of the cold and take a seat in his office. After several minutes of questions and answers, the now ex-sales assistant suggested that he would be starting a new business and requested permission for the wholesale owner to ask these customers to contact him. He explained that he would accumulate several small orders until they were substantial enough, before placing an order with the wholesaler. The business owner agreed to assist and inquired about the new business opening date."

"'Tomorrow morning at 8 am,' he replied, and stood, thanked the owner, turned and departed through the door and down to the street."

"How did he get on?" asked Simon, totally enthralled by the tale.

"That we will learn later," Isaac replied.

"So, how does that help me?" Simon asked.

"A great question to be answered tomorrow when we meet back here on the train," Isaac said and stood and left. Simon looked around to find that the train was still very full and that they had only travelled four stations from when Isaac had boarded. He was unsure how Isaac would answer the question the next day, but he couldn't wait to find out.

Chapter Four

Sure enough, the following afternoon, Isaac boarded the train and took the only seat left in the otherwise full carriage. It was the one next to Simon.

"How do you do that?" Simon asked as Isaac sat.

"How do I do what?" Isaac replied.

"Always get on when this seat is empty?"

"It is not my doing, but yours," he replied. "The people in the carriage don't know it, but they are sensing you are waiting for someone, so they choose another seat or stand and leave this for me." Isaac replied.

Before Simon could even draw a breath to speak, Isaac continued.

"Now, back to answering your question from yesterday. Did you work out the answer?" Isaac asked, clasping his hands together into a ball and resting them in his lap.

"I didn't know I was supposed to answer my own questions," Simon replied.

"Oh, but yes, you will always be answering your own questions, as you already know the answer to them. You just haven't looked inside your head and searched your mind to determine what you should or could do. So, what do you think is the answer to your question?"

Simon was perplexed, to say the least. "I… I don't know," he replied, shaking his head.

"Are you happy with what you are doing currently, and you do know the answer to that?" Isaac said factually.

Simon replied, "No," even before he realised he'd said it.

"A quick answer is more often the truth, as you don't need to consider the ramifications if you are about to lie," Isaac said, the trademark smile on his face. "So, we know you are not happy with your work. What else are you not happy with?" was the following question from Isaac.

Simon thought for some thirty seconds, running through the things in his life that he didn't like or was unhappy with. His life at home was OK, and his friends were great, so what else did he feel he was unhappy with other than his job? He was about to say nothing when another word rolled off his tongue.

"Success," he said, looking around as though someone else had said it, as he felt he hadn't.

"What do you mean by success?" Isaac retorted.

Simon now had to discover why he had said success. He figured his subconscious had conjured up the word, and now he needed to work out why. He thought for a moment. His gut tightened just for a second as he realised, he needed to do more in his life than just be a salesman.

"I need to build something I can be proud of," he explained, looking down at Isaac. This time, there were only seconds of silence. "I have always wanted to build my own business." Simon stopped and took a breath. '*Wow,*' he thought to himself, *where did that all come from?*"

"See, you answered your own question. Progress," Isaac said, standing and heading to the door. He turned as he passed the seat in front of where he had been sitting. "With your next question, I want an answer tomorrow," he said, and turned back to walk with the other departing passengers out onto the platform.

"What question?" Simon said out loud. There was no one left in the carriage to answer.

Chapter Five

Simon headed to work the following morning. He had yet to talk to his wife, Judy, about any of this, as he knew she would only ask more questions, and he still had to figure out what the next question was, let alone the answer. After getting off the train, he headed up to High Street and toward his office.

He had arranged for several clients to meet him over the course of the day so he could demonstrate the new database server that his company was selling. He arrived in the line of the coffee shop next door to his building. He joined the queue and stood, waiting while struggling to formulate the next question.

"Excuse me, are you waiting for your order or are you in the line?" a voice said from behind. Simon looked up and realised the line had moved on, and he was there daydreaming, as usual.

"Shit, sorry… yes, I am in the line," he said over his shoulder as he took the three steps to rejoin back behind the person in front.

Having got his coffee, Simon headed up the five flights of stairs to the top floor where he worked.

"I am going to make sure our next office has a lift," said an overweight man in a poorly fitting suit, coming up behind him.

They arrived together on the landing in front of a polished steel door. The top half was glass, with the company name and logo covering much of the space.

Simon reached out and pushed the door open. "After you, boss," he said, allowing the now red-faced, heavy-breathing man to pass.

As the man passed, he said, "You all set up for the meetings in the board room today. I don't want to see us lose any sales of these new boxes."

Simon was the only salesman who had arranged meetings. The other two were in their respective offices, each on their mobile phones. Simon guessed that neither of them was talking to clients.

Christian was the boss's wife's younger brother, and Phillip was the boss's oldest son. Neither were any good at selling or, for that matter, client relations.

Simon spent the entire day explaining and demonstrating the new server to seven of his best clients. By the end of the day, he had orders from two and commitments to order from four others, with his last demonstration being cut short as the client had an emergency back at his business. He had hurriedly headed out of the demonstration, apologising profusely to Simon as he passed by him.

Simon smiled and replied, "Will call you tomorrow."

The client gave him the thumbs up as he closed the office door.

His boss called him into his office as the last client raced out the door. "What was that all about?" he asked Simon.

Simon didn't get a chance to answer, as his boss assumed that the demo had gone south and the client had left in a huff. "You know I don't want to lose any sales with this new release, and clearly, that demo didn't go well. You need to get him back as soon as possible and close the deal. As for your other clients, I want you to hand the four you have, who have yet to order, over to Christian and Phillip so that you can start looking for some more customers."

Simon was gobsmacked. "So, what about the commission on these four? They have all committed to order." he said.

"Whoever closes the sale gets the commission. You know the policy," his boss said.

"Really?" Simon replied, leaving the boss's office. Returning to his desk, he grabbed the four client files and, disgusted, tossed them onto Phillip's desk. "Here, try closing these," he said and walked back to his office.

It was an hour later than he realised as he headed along High Street to the train station. He boarded the train and stood near the doors, as there were no seats available. The train continued to fill as it passed the London city stations and did not appear to be emptying enough to get a seat the whole trip. Finally, four stops from his station, Simon got a seat. The events of the day were so disappointing to him that he did not spare a single thought for Isaac.

When he got home, he spent the first hour talking with Judy about what had happened at his office and what his boss had made him do. She, as always, listened sympathetically to Simon.

"So, what do you think you should do?" she asked. "Maybe it is time to look for a new job," she added.

Simon had calmed down, and now, for the first time since the previous afternoon, he thought about the question Isaac had alluded to. "Maybe that is what he meant," he said out loud.

"Who?" Judy answered.

Simon, still deep in thought and not even registering that his wife had even asked the question, answered: "Isaac."

"Who the hell is Isaac?" she asked.

Simon snapped back into the present and realised what he had said. "He… he," Simon stammered, trying to think how best to address what had just happened. Composed, he continued, "There is a guy I met on the train, Isaac, and he…" and so he spent the next two hours over dinner explaining the past few days.

"So, I have no idea what the question is I have to answer," he said, more as a question to Judy than a statement.

She looked at him for a few seconds. "Maybe ask him if you should get a new job, and while you are at it, see if this is some sort of scam, as I don't feel comfortable about the whole thing," she said, standing and heading to the kitchen.

Simon sat and contemplated the scam suggestion. After all, he knew Judy was smart and worked long hours as well. Maybe he should consider listening to his wife. He gathered up his now-empty plate and headed into the kitchen to join her. "So enough about me. How was your day?"

Judy was in the process of doing the washing up and, as it happens, was just then thinking about the same new job thing.

Chapter Six

Judy had been working for several years at a large trucking business that had struggled after COVID. Like Simon, she was not appreciated at her workplace. Sure, the other people in the office were great. However, her manager, the business owner and her husband were often rude to her. This often occurred when an issue arose from somewhere in the business, often a problem caused by management, and she would be told, not asked, to fix it.

She had recently discovered a shortfall in some of the parts inventory, as well as money missing from the petty cash draw. Judy had attributed the cash issue in the past to change errors by the office staff, who were often asked to pop out and get milk or items for the kitchen. They would use petty cash to purchase the items and forget to return the change. The problem was that the amount missing was pretty much the same each time, five pounds exactly. As for the parts inventory, she had no idea.

Judy had insisted that a policies and procedures manual be introduced and signed off by all current employees, as well as being a part of the induction procedure for any new employees. She had even found a website offering templates and gone to the trouble of drawing up a sizable document containing all the necessary policies and procedures for the trucking business. She presented this to her direct boss, who said he would run it by the owners. That was six months ago, and even though she had asked him several times if he had heard back, the answer was always, "Not as yet."

Today, she was going to approach the owner directly and inform her of the missing inventory items, as well as ask about the policies and procedures document she was supposed to have received. Judy was not comfortable mentioning the missing items or petty cash problem to her direct manager, as he was one of the people she considered a possible suspect.

She had arrived at work half an hour early, as was her practice. Her manager, on the other hand, always seemed to be half an hour late each day. So, with him not there, she headed upstairs to the executive area.

Arriving at the desk at the top of the stairs, she stood and looked around. Samantha, everyone called her Sam, was not in yet and was PA to both the owner and her husband, the latter of whom was hardly ever in.

Judy knew that Mrs. Miller would be in her office, as her car was in the parking lot. She all but tiptoed down the hall to her office door, which was open. Mrs. Miller was on the phone, so Judy stepped back beside the entrance and was just out of sight of the owner.

As she waited, she started to think this was not such a great idea and turned back towards the stairs, just as Mrs. Miller called out.

"Yes, Judy, how can I help you?" Judy spun and headed back the two paces to the doorway and poked her head in around the corner.

"Um, yes, do you have a minute?" she asked tentatively.

"What is this about? I am very busy," she all but snapped back at the lady now standing in the doorway.

Mrs. Miller's office was not a large room. However, it was, to say the least, a mess. The old wooden desk she sat at was in the centre and at the rear of the space. On the desk were papers, magazines, folders and what could only be called other rubbish.

The wooden chair in front of the desk was likewise covered with a pile of disorganised sheets of paper, so being asked to sit there was not going to happen.

To the right was an old window with a dilapidated Venetian blind that must have been pulled up to three-quarters about one hundred years ago. Under it sat what looked like, and possibly was, a foldaway camping table.

It was also covered with several chaotic piles of bulging manila folders and papers.

Behind her chair, on the wall, was a painting or poster of a very large Mack truck.

Judy took a pace forward. She had been in the room for whatever reason many times over the years and never understood how this woman managed to function in such a mess. She knew that it was Sam who worked tirelessly to keep this failing company together.

"I was wondering if I could have a few minutes of your time to go over a couple of rather sensitive issues I have discovered?" Judy said as she moved a little closer to the chair in front of the desk.

"What issues?" Mrs. Miller asked in a bored tone as she reached for a dirty old coffee mug, precariously sitting atop several folders.

Judy spent the next few minutes explaining what she had discovered and placed the relevant documents over the top of the chair and onto a large pile of what looked like printed emails.

Mrs Miller, bored, scanned the half-dozen pages and, without looking up, said, "So how are you planning to fix this?"

"It is not about fixing it. It is discovering who is not returning monies to the petty cash and where the inventory items are going," Judy replied.

"Are you suggesting someone is stealing these things?" Mrs. Miller snapped.

Judy was certain that the items were being stolen; however, she needed to gather more evidence to substantiate her claim.

"No, not yet. However, I think that the Policies and Procedures documents that Peter said he had given you would go a very long way in keeping track of a lot of things in the business."

Mrs. Miller stood, and Judy jumped a step back. "Firstly, young lady, you have not answered my question, and second, I have received no information about implementing any policies or practices, as you mentioned. Now, are you suggesting that the money and inventory items are being stolen?"

Judy wished she had not come up here and decided not to correct Mrs Miller's mistake; however, she knew she was right and continued to stand her ground. "As I said, Mrs. Miller, I don't have enough evidence on both matters. I am here to inform you that this occurred, and I have put forward a suggestion on how to prevent further similar situations. If Peter has not presented my policy and procedure documents," Judy said putting a emphasis on Procedures, "then I am more than happy to get you a copy now."

"I am not interested in policies and procedures. We have had the same procedures for the past ten years, and they seem to be working fine. As for the missing items and money, they are your problem. Now, go back downstairs and find them. Plus, I will have a word with

Peter when he gets in," and with that, Mrs. Miller sat and picked up the phone receiver and started to dial.

Judy got the hint and turned to leave the office. *'I need to find a new job,'* she thought as she passed Sam's still-empty desk.

"Just a normal day," Judy answered to Simon's question.

Chapter Seven

It was Friday morning, and Simon hadn't slept much the previous night. As the day wore on, he felt increasingly troubled both about what had happened the day before, as well as about what Isaac both expected of him and whether he was, in fact, legitimate.

When he arrived in the office, the first thing he did was check the system for new orders.

None.

He headed past Philip's office and could not see the client folders anywhere on his desk.

Next, he headed past Christian's office and noted the four folders sitting atop his in-tray, untouched.

By the time Simon had finished, it was after six pm in the now-empty office. His day had been a success, with his five new orders in hand. These he would put into the system on Monday morning. As he headed to the train station, it was getting dark. He figured Isaac would have long gone and was surprised when he got on at Earl's Court. Again, even though the train was standing room only, the seat next to Simon was empty. Isaac made his way down the aisle and sat down next to him.

Simon leaned closer to Isaac and whispered, "Could we wait until the train empties a bit? I would prefer to discuss this matter privately, without others overhearing."

"You needn't worry," Isaac replied in his normal soft and calm voice. "They can't hear you."

With that, Simon sat back in disbelief and asked the same question again, only louder so people standing next to Isaac and in the two seats in front could hear. Not one person so much as glanced in his direction, nor did anyone seem to be listening.

"Who the hell are you?" Simon asked in a level that anyone within two meters would have heard.

"Asked and answered," replied Isaac, a smile once again lighting up his face.

"Yes, but how do you do that?" Simon continued. "Sitting on a crowded train and not having anyone hear us?"

Isaac just sat there, staring up at him.

Simon just shook his head.

"And I don't have a question for you either," he added. "Ah, but you do," said Isaac, not even allowing a quarter-second to pass from when Simon finished talking.

Simon sat bewildered, to say the least. His mind was

racing. 'I don't have a question,' he thought, 'so what is he on about? I am not going to ask if he is legit, as clearly, if he can do the seat and silence thing, then he is not about to scam me. So, what the hell am I supposed to ask?'

He looked back over to Isaac, who sat smiling up at him, clearly waiting for a question. Then, looking back out the black window, *'OK,'* Simon thought. *'A question. Will I ask if I should get a new job? Yes, that's it.'*

He turned back to Isaac. "Should I get a new job?"

Without so much as a blink, Isaac replied. "Wrong question!"

Simon was now totally perplexed. There has been no other question that he and Judy had discussed. So that ruled that out. There was nothing at the office that he had discussed with Isaac that would raise a question.

He looked at Isaac again and raised his hands. "I give up. What is my question?"

Isaac took a short breath. "I know you never give up."

Now think, *'How the hell would he know that about me?'* Simon thought. He tried to remember what had been said in the previous two meetings. Very little was the first memory.

"The story," he said softly to Isaac and noted a glimmer in his dark eyes.

Simon ran the story through his mind, and after about two more stops, he turned his gaze from the window back to Isaac. "Should I start my own business?"

Isaac stood and walked away down the now-empty

aisle. "I need your answer to your question tomorrow," he said, stepping out onto the Holborn station platform.

"But it's Saturday," he said out loud.

The lady in front of him turned and said, "No dear, it's Friday today."

Simon woke the next morning and got ready with the shopping list, as it was his job to do the grocery shopping. It was easier to jump a bus to the Spires shopping mall, as parking was always impossible on weekends.

The bus arrived, and Simon jumped on, then climbed the stairs to the top deck. He sat up towards the front and settled in for the twenty-minute ride via the hospital and train station, to the mall.

He had rested his mind about the Isaac question and was back in his daydreaming mode. Looking out the window, he came back to the present and realised the bus was pulling out from the hospital stop.

Looking forward, he noticed in the reflection on the front glass of two people coming up the stairs behind him. The first sat just over to his right, and the second settled in beside him.

Simon turned and almost screamed in shock as he looked across at Isaac. "How…" he started to whisper but stopped, then looked around and back to Isaac.

"Can they hear me?" he asked.

"Well, sort of, but more as mumbling," Isaac replied.

"So, what is the answer to your question?" not giving Simon a chance to say anything else.

"Hell, I don't know for sure. I haven't really thought about it."

"Yes, you have; you have been thinking about it for most of your working life," commented Isaac.

Simon, taken aback by this comment, seemed to answer without thinking, blurting out, "Yes," and putting his hand up to his mouth to stop any other unthought words from being emitted.

"Great and good answer," Isaac said. Then continued, "You are starting to see how this works. If you have a question, you cannot answer, or, for that matter, don't know what question you need to answer, I will help. Now, get to work and start your new business. And by the way, you'd best get off; this is your stop."

Simon looked back out the window, and sure enough, the bus was slowing in front of the shopping mall. He grabbed his shopping bags and headed down the stairs and just made it out the door as the bus started to pull away from the stop. He turned to wave to Isaac, but he must have moved, as he was no longer in the seat.

Chapter Eight

It was Monday morning as Simon walked along King Street to the office again, having slept little the two nights earlier. He had answered the next question while he was doing the grocery shopping. What the hell am I going to do? He figured it had to be in sales, and it had to involve computers, as that was what he seemed to know best. His following two questions, he knew, were a lot harder to answer and had kept him awake most of the night. When and how?

The 'when' answer came quicker than he had imagined.

Having just arrived at work, the boss called him into his office.

Simon went to sit. "No need to sit," the boss started. "I thought I told you to give both Phillip and Christian two each of your customers.

"You chose, however, to give them all to Christian, and the poor man was here till all hours Friday night and has spent the weekend slaving over them, but as of this morning, he has yet to close them but is certain he will have it done by this afternoon."

This floored Simon. When he left on Friday, both Christian and Phillip were already gone, and most of Simon's day had been spent on phone calls and sending quotes to the four clients, who were apparently now assigned to Christian, not Phillip. All the clients had been asking questions, and all four gave Simon 100% commitment to have the quote Simon had sent them, with their official order attached and signed on Monday, today.

"Are you serious?" Simon said, loud enough for the entire office to hear. "Neither Christian nor Phillip could close the top on a box of Smarties, let alone close a hundred-thousand-pound computer deal."

"I beg your pardon," the boss said, standing from his chair. "How dare you speak to me like that, and how dare you talk about Christian and Phillip or, for that matter, any of my staff in that manner! I think it is time…"

Simon put up his hand, "yes I agree it is time, and in fact, well past it."

He spun on his heel and walked out of the office, then across the hall into his office, where he picked up his suitcase, laptop, and the thumb drive next to it, and headed out the door. No one saw the latter item.

It was just after ten in the morning by the time Simon had arrived home. He set up his laptop on the table in the spare bedroom and, by just after 2 p.m. had orders from all four clients to whom Christian had supposedly spoken. In addition, a massive order for two new servers from the last client, who had hurried out the door the day of the demonstrations. Simon informed all clients that he would be taking the orders under the banner of his new company.

All the clients happily agreed to confirm this understanding via email. It appeared that none of them had ever heard of a Christian or Phillip in the company where he had worked. Likewise, all clients were glad they would no longer be ordering from the company where Simon was no longer a contractor. That was the easy part. Now, he had to convince the supplier to allow him to purchase almost half a million pounds of equipment with only a little over five thousand and change in their joint bank account.

Chapter Nine

Simon considered whether he had overextended himself and reviewed any legal implications of taking on clients. He checked his contract from when he started at the old computer company and did not find any non-compete agreements, which was a positive step. He made a note on his to-do list to ensure future employment contracts included a non-compete clause. His focus returned to the issue of financing. The possibility of mortgaging the house was not viable, as he and his wife, Judy, had agreed when buying the house that this would never happen. Therefore, it was not an option.

The following morning, Simon headed to The Office Works at Uxbridge. He arrived at Cowley Mill Road to find the place packed with cars. After a further search down the road, he found a parking space and once he parked, he headed into The Office Works. As he entered the store, he was taken aback by the number of people milling around the tables and the many aisles of office supplies. He made his way to the stationary aisle only to find it the busiest of the lot. Having obtained a trolley, he started to pack it with pens, notepads, and all the items he recalled using in his previous job.

"Looks like you are starting a new business?" a voice said from behind him.

Simon was focused on trying to pick the best stapler and just answered, "Yes, is it that easy to tell?"

The person who had spoken didn't reply and just stood behind Simon. As he turned, Simon bumped the man and apologised. "Oops, sorry."

"No problem," the man said.

Simon looked down. It was Isaac.

"Oh, my goodness, what are you doing here?" Simon asked, dropping the stapler and staples into his trolley.

"You have a question, and since I will most likely not be seeing you on the Piccadilly line any time soon, I just thought it best to come see you."

Simon was, to say the least, surprised beyond belief. 'How the hell did Isaac know he had quit, know he would be here, and know he had a question?'

"What question?" he asked, deciding he would never get the other questions answered.

"Money," replied Isaac. "You can answer the question across the road at the café, and don't forget printer cartridges," he said as he turned and headed out and across the road.

Simon completed his shopping and loaded his car. He then proceeded to the small cafe, located only two cars away from where he had parked.

"Regarding your inquiry about finances, allow me to help with your answer," he began. "Do you recall the individual I mentioned who had resigned from his job and embarked on his own business venture?"

Simon reflected for a moment and remembered the story. "Yes," he responded.

"Well," continued Isaac, "he was in a similar situation as you. After visiting several bookstores, he found a small book that he thought would help. By the time he finished reading, he had discovered four important things to do." Finishing the sentence, Isaac looked at Simon. "You purchased a notebook, didn't you?"

Simon took a moment to consider whether this was part of the story, or in fact, a question. As Isaac had only sat there after saying it, Simon figured it was, in fact, a question.

"Oh, yes, I did," said Simon, then he jumped up, raced out to the car and retrieved the said notebook and a new pen to boot. He returned to his seat and opened the notepad to the last page. He then looked up at Isaac. It was Simon who smiled.

"Hmm, I will answer my own question," Isaac said looking at Simon holding the book open and then continued with the answer. "I see you opened it on the last page. Clearly, you have worked out that I am about to give you a list, and lists need to be readily accessible, so back of the notebook?"

Simon just continued to mimic Isaac and sat smiling. His head, however, was still working, amazed at the abilities of this man.

Isaac then began list the important things that the man in the story had discovered, while Simon started to write.

"Firstly, find a good accountant. You would never want to employ them but rather keep them as the outside, third-party checkers of your books, and, in these early days, give you help in setting up your business."

"Second, very important thing. Ten per cent of all you earn is yours to keep.[1] The remainder goes back into the business."

"Third, stay with what you know and understand, and don't take on something someone has told you will be great for your business, if you don't know anything about it."

"Finally, friends or family never make good business partners or employees."

---

1. Quote from the book by George S. Calson (2008) *The Richest Man in Babylon.* Signet. (Original work published 1926)

Isaac stopped and looked across the table at Simon. As usual, Simon had worked out that a smile from Isaac meant he was expecting an answer, question, or comment. The only thing that came to his mind was a question. "So how does this help with my money problem?"

Isaac just continued to smile.

'Well, I'm not getting an answer to that question,' Simon thought. "Ok, I will go find an accountant." he said.

"First thing, I would suggest, as you don't want to lose those orders," Isaac responded as he stood and headed out of the cafe.

Simon put his hands over his face and said out loud to the full café, "How does he know?"

He spent the rest of the morning researching local accountants. He knew his wife's brother was a very good one, but the words from Isaac came back each time he looked for an easy way out.

'No friends or family'.

Finally settling on one and having spoken with her for the best part of an hour, he agreed to meet.

Simon headed off to meet with his new accountant. They agreed to make this an informal meeting with the primary goal of facilitating the necessary cross flow of information. She needed his business information to set up a new client in her system and for Simon to discover what he needed to have in place at his end to collect the necessary tax information.

By the time Simon returned to his new home office, it

was pushing 3 p.m., and he still had no way of funding the orders. He decided to call the supplier and ask if he could get a thirty-day account or maybe push his luck for a sixty-day one. The wholesale owner called the country manager, and he reported back that this was a no-go, and cash with order was the only accepted way with a new account.

Simon was still very concerned and asked Judy if she would consider revising their agreement to mortgage the house. She responded negatively, explaining that they had agreed not to do so for an apparent reason: mortgaging the house and using that money for any business venture carries the risk of losing both the house and still owing the money. Therefore, she advised Simon to seek alternative solutions.

It was the end of the working day when the phone rang. It was the business owner who had had to leave the server demonstration early, as well as the now being Simons new client with the biggest order in the pipeline.

"Hi Simon, how is the delivery date coming for the two servers? I need them by the end of the month, and I sure don't want to have to go back to your old boss for them."

Not wanting to lie, Simon came back to him. "As I am sure you can imagine, finance for these orders is taking a little longer than expected; however, I will get back to you…" he said, looking up at the clock on the back wall. It was five-thirty. "By five pm or earlier tomorrow, hopefully with the information that stops both of us from changing the status quo."

"Great, and I look forward to your call."

Simon, likewise, hung up and then dropped his head into his palm. "Shit, shit, how the hell will I do this."

He couldn't sleep; he needed an answer. He had got out of bed, not wanting to disturb Judy, and headed to the office, located at the other end of the hall. Arriving at the wall mirror outside the entrance to the office, he stopped and looked at himself.

"What could have Isaac said that I missed?" he said to his reflection and continued, "He usually either gives me a question to answer or tells me if I have a question. In both cases, I will most likely know the answer. So, I have a question, what the hell is the answer?"

He remained there, looking at himself, almost expecting the reflection to take on its own life and answer, "Yes, I know," but that was not going to happen. He stood back and turned right, and his reflection turned left, and both headed to the office.

He sat and did as Isaac had said. If you have a question, look within yourself for the answer. Time ticked by, and all his head did was to keep reminding him he was about to lose the orders to his old boss.

"OK, head, that is not going to happen," he said out loud. Let me think.

'I met with Isaac. He gave me the list; I asked him there

and then, how does that help with my money problem? and then Isaac just smiled'.

Simon then went on to the next part of the meeting, but something stopped him. He smiled, thinking again. 'He smiled; he didn't say 'wrong question'. His mind released the thought and then moved on to the next part of the meeting.

"The answer is in here somewhere," he now said aloud. Thinking still about the conversation he recalled in his mind the next question he had asked, *'Should I get an accountant, and he said yes and quickly'.*

"That's it, I need to ask the accountant," Simon said again, out loud to his empty office.

First thing that morning, at nine a.m., Simon called his new accountant, and her advice was simple. Approach the supplier with the orders and suggest that the supplier invoice the client directly at Simon's quoted price. Then, pay Simon's new company the margin on the cost price. Then, agree with the supplier that once the deals are all done and paid for, in full, the supplier allows Simon's company to have a 30-day credit account.

Simon, on the other hand, must, the accountant had stressed to him, have all his clients on a cash-on-supply basis, not a 30-day account. If they did not agree to this, then he would have to ask them to go elsewhere for supplies. She explained that her small business clients found that if they could offer something unique, then the clients would in most cases accept these terms.

'Unique,' Simon had thought at the time. *'I buy and sell computers, as do my competitors. How can I make that unique?'*

The problem rested with him for the next hour. He thought back over his time at the old job in High Street.

"Wow!" he exclaimed. "It was only a few days ago and already it is, my old job," *'Why did he do so well with such a shitty operation?'* he asked himself.

He was learning fast that what Isaac had said seemed to be working. He knew he knew the answer; he just needed to stand back and look for the answer in his head.

'For starters,' he thought, *'I was the best and only salesman in the business. That does not help as I am the only salesman in this business. Price,'* he went on in his head, *'My products could be the cheapest, and that is an advantage. We used to lower the price to crazy levels to win a deal, but all that did was win the deal, and anyone can lower the price. Is that unique?'* He asked himself.

'Additionally, this is a new business, and I need a margin to cover expenses and keep the business afloat.'

He recalled that during his conversation with his new accountant, she mentioned that ninety per cent of new startups fail mainly due to cash flow issues.

"Not me. So unique, what?" he again, said out loud.

Simon set up his new office in the spare bedroom and put the new stationery items in their correct places. Finally, after an hour, he stood at the doorway into the room and smiled.

"My new office and boardroom to my new company," he said, as the phone on his new desk rang. He all but ran the three metres and scooped it up.

Looking at the screen, he sighed. The accountant, was the two words he had in for the contact for this number. He was not sure how to spell her name at the time, and now that he knew it, he had not bothered to change the entry.

'Later,' he thought as he answered.

The conversation was short and as he finished and put the phone down, he again smiled. He now had a company name registered both nationally and internationally and he was now the sole director of ComShift.

"Wow, this lady is good. Her customer service is top level. She is a keeper."

His phone dinged, and he again picked it up to see he had a new email. It was from the accountant.

Hi Simon,

Thanks again for this great opportunity to represent your new company, ComShift. I trust that the name is to your liking. I was looking for a name that would best describe what you do, helping people and companies get the best computing needs seems to be just that, moving computers. I have also supplied a logo you may like. Please let me know if this is not what you wanted, and I will cancel the registration process.

In the meantime, you will need to open a bank account

in the company name with you as the director and secretary. I have sent you several DocuSign documents with all the necessary forms for the new company. Please sign these, and once completed, the document will automatically be returned to me.

Also attached is an itemised invoice for my time to date and registration costs, etc. Please revise this document, and if you are satisfied with it, proceed with payment as per the details provided at the bottom of the invoice.

Again, thank you for this opportunity.,
Yours sincerely
Your new Accountant 😊

Simon completed the DocuSign process, and after printing the other forms and the invoice, he placed them on his desk. He then pulled out his brand-new 'To-Do List' pad and added the first item. Get a new filing cabinet.

He placed the to-do pad on his desk and moved his hand back over to his phone. As he was about to file the email from the accountant, he hesitated. Something in his head said no. Not sure what 'No' meant, he just sat looking down at the phone. He re-read the words. He had done all that was asked of him, so why not file the email? He had learned from his old job that all emails must be filed, as you never know when you will need to refer to them, so that was not the issue. Something was bugging him about the email, so he printed it on the new printer. He read the printed copy. Still no answer, so he placed it on top of the to-do pad.

"I need to get these orders sorted," he said to his reflection on the black laptop screen.

Simon compiled the five orders into a single large order for the supplier. Next, he went about making up an invoice for the commission of fifteen per cent with all the necessary information, including the Logo for ComShift.

It was 4.30 p.m. when he printed out the invoice and then the order, which also featured the logo at the top. He then checked his to-do list and noted that he had to call his client with the order for two systems, by five with an answer. He didn't have one. As was his rule, he called him anyway, and after advising him that he would be talking directly to the country manager he would have an answer in the morning.

He was aware that the supplier would not be open; nonetheless, he possessed the direct contact information for Michael, the country manager at Dell.

"Hi Simon, I was expecting your call," Michael said before Simon could even say hello.

"Say what?" Simon said, totally surprised.

"Yup," Michael continued. "Your old boss," he said with a chuckle, "called and told me you quit, and I was not to speak to you or, under any circumstances, take any orders from you. So, my first question to you is, why the hell did it take you so long to quit? And before you answer that, I need to know when I can expect to receive the first order." Michael was now laughing.

"Oh my God," Simon started. "Did he call? Really?"

"Yes, just this morning. When did you quit?"

"Well, for starters, I did quit a few days ago, but only seconds before he was about to fire me. As for the order, I don't have one." Now, it was Simon's turn to chuckle. "I have five, but there is a big problem,"

There was a pause. Finally, Michael came back on the line. "Five. was all that he said?"

"Yes, five. And they will be from a company called ComShift."

Again, there was a long pause. Simon could hear Michael typing on his computer.

"We don't have a reseller by that name. How did you get a job there so fast?" Michael asked.

"Yes, I know there is no reseller in your system by that name and therein lies the problem."

"Firstly, I got the job this afternoon when my new accountant registered ComShift Pty. Ltd. with me as Sole Director and Secretary." As there was no response from the other end, he continued. "As for the five orders, they total close to half a million pounds, and that is also a problem."

Finally, a voice emanated from the other participant in the conversation. "Shit, that is a problem!" Was all he could say.

"What, the problem ComShift is not a reseller or the size of the order?"

"Both." Michael replied, and the line went silent again.

It was close to midnight when Simon hung-up the call.

Simon had explained the method suggested by his accountant for mitigating the financial risk associated with such a large sum, as for the company becoming a reseller, that was Michaels's doing. After several emails to head office in America and the threat that the competition may well obtain the orders if ComShift did not become a reseller, the five orders were locked into the system. Simon just made seventy-five thousand pounds in commission. At least he would once the clients all paid the supplier. This was his total annual retainer for his old job.

Chapter Ten

The following morning, after the first full night's sleep in ages, Simon dressed and headed to his new office. The first thing was to finish setting up his website and email addresses. *'So, let's get real,'* he thought.

'I will have an email address of The.Director@ComShift.com.uk.'

His new accountant had applied for and got the DNS for his business, so Simon entered the address into the hosting site and paid for a twelve-month email subscription. He then went back into his email app and set up the address.

"All done," he said to the empty office. "Now let's see if it all works."

There was a ding sound that came from the laptop. He checked the web page he had open for the hosting site, and it showed no change. Then he noticed that the email app icon had an envelope sitting on top of it. What the hell, I haven't even sent an email to myself to test if it is working. He clicked on and called the email app to the front. Sure enough, there was an email in the inbox. It was from yourfriend@outhere.com.

Simon started shaking his head.

"No one has my email address. No, no, not Spam. Surely not."

He was not going to open it just in case it was some sort of Trojan horse or worse, a ransom email. He opened his internet security app, something his accountant insisted he purchase. He had it do a full check of the computer and found that it could also check the email. All was clear. With his heart rate rising, he opened the email. His mouth fell open.

"How?" he said, throwing his hands in the air.

Good morning, Simon

I assume you checked my email for malware and the like. Well done. Never trust an unknown address. Likewise, I have a few points regarding your email setup.

I suggest you delete your director email address, as you are inviting trouble from companies trolling for MDs, CFOs, and any other decision-maker types.

I assume you have purchased several addresses that you can use. You need one for you, clearly. So just your first name, and surname initial, all in lowercase, then the @ComShift. That way, as you grow, you have a simple but effective email address policy.

Include an info@ address, and at this stage, it will be you checking it. When you hire an office person, they will be responsible for monitoring it. You don't want every email coming to you.

I would also like to congratulate you on your first order. I imagine the profit is substantial. Remember, you MUST NOT call it profit till it is sitting in your bank account as cleared funds. On that point, how are you placed for a coffee at 10 am this morning?

Good.

I will meet you then at Tea & Toast at New Barnet, just down from the Shell Garage.

Your Friend

Isaac

Simon read the email a second time. He needed to be sure it was real, and that someone had not been logged into his computer this whole time. He had done a quick Ctrl-Alt-Del and checked in the task manager that he was the only user logged in. He looked at his watch. 9:15 am. He knew the coffee shop as he got his hair cut across the road from the garage. He guessed Isaac already knew this.

Chapter Eleven

He arrived five minutes before ten am. There were no parking spaces as he drove along Barnet Road. He did a U-turn at Victoria Road and headed back towards the café. As he approached, a car pulled out from in front of the Tea & Toast. Simon just shook his head as he drove into the vacant space.

As he entered, Isaac was sitting alone on the leather lounge just inside the door.

"Good parking spot," Isaac said as Simon walked past, heading to the counter to order.

"No, no," Isaac said, waving Simon to come back. "All ordered. Your normal flat white, extra hot and one sugar. Plus, I got us a piece of chocolate cake each. Hope you don't mind."

Simon sat and just stared at this man. "Why me?" he asked.

Isaac smiled. Simon now totally understood the smile treatment.

There would be no reply to the question and more than likely; there was to be a more appropriate question instead. Simon thought for a moment.

"Thank you for the email suggestions. I have sent you my new address and listed the other addresses that you can use as well."

"Thanks," was all Isaac said, and he resumed the smile position. Simon then pulled the next question that he had thought of while Isaac had answered the previous one.

"So, where to from here?"

"You still have not answered your own question. One that your accountant posed, indirectly, when you spoke to her."

Simon thought back to the conversation with his new accountant. "I have the software, MYOB, that she suggested. The company name and DNS are all squared away. Security software is loaded and hopefully working. Bank and accounts all set up." he paused. "No, not sure what else," he finished as the waitress placed a steaming large mug of very hot coffee in front of him.

"Did you add sugar?" Simon politely asked her.

"No, sorry, I forgot. You can help yourself over there," she replied and pointed to a space at the end of the counter.

Simon looked around behind her and noted the serviettes, sugar and sauces all sitting on the counter surface.

"Wow! Great customer service. Not!" he said quietly to Isaac as he stood and headed to the counter.

When he returned, Isaac took another sip of his tea, then he sat up and, looking at Simon, said, "Do you recall our friend who started his sporting equipment business?"

Simon did not answer, assuming it to be a rhetorical question. The assumption was proved correct as Isaac continued.

"Similar to your situation, our colleague was offering products to customers who had multiple options regarding their purchases. One of those potential clients had called him and asked if he could supply several brands of tennis rackets. He spent the rest of the day calling other suppliers as his supplier only held three of the brands that the client wanted. By day's end, he had found two other brands from a supplier in France. The last brand the client had requested was unknown to any of the companies he had spoken to. An extensive search of the internet also yielded no results."

"He finally contacted the customer at ten minutes to five p.m. as he had told the customer he would call him before five. When the client answered, our friend explained his findings and provided some tentative pricing for the different products, along with various volume discounts. Finally, he expounded that he was unable to discover anyone who had heard of the brand he had failed to find.

"The client thanked him for his efforts and said he would continue to search for a single supplier who could supply all the brands. Our friend not wanting to give up, asked if the potential client would be happy for him to continue looking for the elusive brand. Having agreed to his request our friend requested the client's email address, then said, 'I will do my best and will call you tomorrow at eleven a.m. with my results.'"

"With that, the client again thanked him and hung up."

Simon was clearly absorbing the story and taking notes, so Isaac continued. "Just a minute had passed when our friend's phone rang. Seeing it was the same number, he answered."

"'Hello, it's me,' said the caller. 'Why did you say you'd call me at eleven a.m.? Do you know where to get the rackets and have other buyers?'"

"'No, no, not at all,' our friend replied."

Isaac paused briefly and looked at Simon before continuing,

"Our friend said, 'I specified eleven a.m. because I wanted to avoid any ambiguity about when I would be calling. If I had said I would call later tomorrow, what time would you have expected my call? Moreover,' he continued without waiting for a response, 'if I had used terms like "early," "soon," or "shortly," you might have been left waiting all day. In the absence of my call, you could have concluded that I was either uninterested in your business or unable to find a supplier for the racket. Therefore, I always provide a specific time to call, regardless of whether I have an answer or not. This also allows us to coordinate if you happen to have a meeting at the scheduled time. Is 11 a.m. tomorrow still convenient for you?' our friend asked."

"After the client had confirmed the time and hung up, our friend began trying to find the racket supplier or manufacturer."

"So, did he find it?" Simon asked.

"Wrong question and not the point," Isaac replied.

"It was close to midnight when our friend finished drafting his quote for all the brands. And yes, he found the manufacturer. It turned out that, as the product was made in Russia, the translation of the name into English had been incorrect."

"At eleven a.m. the following morning, he called the new client. 'Good morning, I hope you had a pleasant evening. I have some very good news. If you check your email...' He ceased his end of the conversation as he could hear the person on the other end typing. Before he could explain that he had found the manufacturer, the client just said 'Wow,' then again. 'Wow,' as he was clearly reading the quote. The wowing stopped."

"Our friend knew from his past sales training that when you are selling, you wait. After all, you have one mouth and two ears, so use them in that ratio, he recalled. Over time, he had become very comfortable with silence. The first person to talk, must be the buyer. A minute passed, then the client said, 'When can I expect delivery?'

"Seeing it was time to close the deal, our friend asked. 'Give me a date and delivery address with your order, and I will do everything in my power to get them to you on time. Do we have a deal?'"

"The answer was yes. And the next question from our friend also needed an answer. 'Do you mind me asking? You hardly know me, and this is a sizable order. Why did you choose to do business with me?'"

"'Fair question. The answer will be included with the formal PO.' The line went dead."

Simon was about to speak but bit his tongue. He needed a moment to compose what he was about to say. He knew it needed to be an answer, not a question. He was learning.

Isaac just sat and sipped his now-cold tea.

"No sense in me asking what the client wrote in the email?"

Isaac just continued to fill his cup with the lukewarm tea still in the pot.

'Yup, got that one right,' Simon thought.

A minute passed before Isaac spoke. "Let me know the answer tomorrow when you purchase our coffee. By the way, I prefer plain black tea in a pot," he added as he exited the room and turned right towards Victoria Road.

Simon sat for a moment before standing and rushing to the door. He called out, after looking right, "What time?"

But there was no one there.

Chapter Twelve

Arriving home from the coffee shop, Simon went straight to his bedroom before heading into his new office. He was about to remove his business shirt when the phone rang. It was Isaac.

"Hi Simon, I did mean to say thank you at our meeting, for being in your business attire. I was happy to see you dressed the way you were. As working from home becomes increasingly common, it is evident that individuals who maintain their usual routines, as if they were commuting to their regular workplace, tend to be significantly more productive in their home office. Furthermore, increased productivity often correlates with greater success."

After the goodbye pleasantries, Simon just stood in front of his bed and once again shook his head. Still wearing the shirt, he headed to the office.

He checked his email and, for once, was glad there were no emails from Isaac. There was, however, an email from his supplier.

Hi Simon,

Congratulations on the new company, and thanks for forwarding your email address this morning. I have some good news. We have delivery dates from the head office for all your equipment. In addition, head office has asked me to pass on their congratulations as well.

On a sad note, I received a phone call this morning from your old boss. He had discovered that you had received orders from his clients. I explained both, what you had told me about the absence of a non-compete clause and that, as a contractor and not an employee, you have every right to maintain your clients. He has cancelled his contract with us and is threatening legal action. I wished him luck on both his future business and the legal action.

So, on a happy note, you have our full support.
Kind regards
Your supplier.

Simon spent the next hour emailing his clients about delivery dates and informing them his supplier would invoice them. As promised, he called his client with the two-server order and confirmed things were all in hand

and he would be getting an email with the invoice and the expected delivery date. He then informed, also via emails, all clients of his new situation, giving them the option to continue with him or stay with his old company.

He knew only too well that talking negatively about a competitor is nearly always a fatal mistake. This includes your old places of employment.

The next morning, he prepared for his ten a.m. meeting with Isaac by reviewing the necessary answers. Clearing his desk, he picked up his to-do list and notebook. Still on his desk was the printed email from his accountant. He started to read it again. After the first paragraph, he paused and stared at it.

Thanks again for this great opportunity to represent your new company, ComShift. I trust that the name suits you well. I was looking for a name that would best describe what you do and helping people and companies meet their best computing needs seems to be just that - moving computers. Please let me know if this is not what you wanted, and I will cancel the registration process.

What was it about this email that bothered him?

Frustrated about what the question was that Isaac needed and knowing he had the original filed on his phone, he screwed it up and threw it in the bin beside the desk. Then he opened his note pad and started to write:

Questions for Isaac

Why did he choose the friend's business?

What is my uniqueness?

Answers……………..

He stopped writing.

After getting a coffee and returning to his desk, he continued to write.

Answer to 1.

a. The customer liked how he got back to him.

b. The client loved how he used specific callback times, AND he always called back on time or earlier.

c. Using words like soon, shortly, tomorrow and other subjective words is not good when planning a call or meeting. The customer liked that.

Answer to 2.

a. Price… not an ongoing advantage or unique

b. Answer the phone and get back to clients… Other resellers do that

c. Deliver a good product on time…same as above

d. Dress well…not sure. not unique

e. The customer is always right… good practice but not unique

Simon took a sip of his coffee. After grimacing and shaking his head as he swallowed the bitter liquid, he remarked, "I forgot the sugar."

"The man had an appointment at nine a.m. with a representative for a potential new supplier of engine parts. It was 8:45 a.m. when the man's wife had called, and it was now just five minutes till his meeting. His PA, who sat out front, had heard the call and asked if she needed to call his driver to the front. He thanked her and then closed his door, making a call."

"It was five minutes past when the representative arrived for his meeting."

"'Good morning,' the PA. said to the rep. 'How can I help you?'"

"'Good morning, yes, I have a meeting with the owner at nine a.m.,' he replied."

"Knowing that her boss was very strict about punctuality, she lied, saying that her boss was no longer in the office."

"'But I had an appointment with him.'"

"'Yes, you said at nine a.m. and it is now five past nine.'"

"'Hell, I am only five minutes late. I am sorry. When will he be back?' He asked, in a rather demeaning and rude manner."

"My colleague had completed his call and opened his door and was about to check if his nine o'clock had arrived when he heard the entire conversation. He was heading down the hall when what the P.A. said next stopped him in his tracks."

"'Do you have a mobile phone?' she asked."

"'Yes,' the rep replied, holding it up and screwing up his face then said, 'doesn't everyone?'"

"'And how long ago did you know what time you would be arriving, maybe a little after nine?'"

"'I...' was all he got out as the P.A. continued."

"'I would guess maybe at least half an hour ago.'"

"'You have a mobile phone. You should have called me and told me you could be ten minutes late due to traffic and would that be OK, even though the more likely reason was you just got up late.'"

"The rep went to reply. The P.A. put up her hand, suggesting he not respond."

"'Either way, a phone call asking if being ten minutes late would be OK, and me saying yes, it is OK, would mean you would now be five minutes early.'"

"She continued. 'Let me ask you another question. How long should my boss have waited, not knowing when you would arrive, and knowing his wife had just gone into the hospital?' Not giving a reason for the wife's issue, she said. 'You tell me, should he have waited one minute?' She looked at the now clearly angry man... '2 minutes, 5 minutes, hell, maybe he should have waited all day, as he or I had no idea when you were arriving. If ever.'"

"The man looked down at her."

"'Hell, lady, I said I was sorry. Can you please do your job and tell me when he will be able to see me?'"

"The boss arrived at her desk."

"'I would suggest never. How dare you speak to my staff that way? I will email your boss to inform him we will be looking elsewhere for the parts.' Turning to head back to his office, he told his PA, 'Let Jamie know I will be down shortly.'"

"How long should I have waited, Simon?" Isaac queried.

Simon sat and reflected. "I apologise for not calling."

He was about to mention that he didn't have Isaac's number, as it had never stayed on his phone any time after Isaac had called him. Considering the situation, Simon knew asking 'how could he have let Isaac know of his delay,' was a question. After a moment, he provided an answer: "I could have called the cafe and asked them to relay a message. Alternatively, I could have left for this meeting earlier to account for any parking issues."

Isaac smiled with satisfaction. It was a smile reminiscent of a parent's pride when their child takes their first step. "Well done," he said. "Now, incorporate this information into your answer you are about to give me." Once more, his face displayed a proud expression.

"Customer Service," Simon said as if he had just told his parents he had been selected for Oxford.

"Explain?" Isaac asked.

"Price does not make me unique. Selling the same as others does not make me unique. As I just sell products manufactured by others. The one tool I have and can excel with is customer service. I sell products manufactured by a third party and like with our friend in the story, my main differentiator is providing excellent customer service. My accountant alluded to that in an email. It took me till this morning to see it.

Simon sat and smiled. "Now can I go and buy us some beverages, from the not-so-good customer service people?" he said and headed to the counter.

"I need more information when you return," Isaac replied as Simon passed by him.

On his return, Simon was about to ask the logical question, however he decided to expand on his previous answer and write it all into the back of his notebook.

"OK, he started to say and write, the things at my disposal to be better than our competitors are:" Simon then listed off things.

- Honesty
- Punctuality
- Discipline
- Understanding communication. This includes following up with clients every time you say or communicate that you will. Included in this is that not only will you call back or reply electronically, but you will also do so either at or before a specified time, regardless of whether you have an answer or not.

- Dress and always appear and behave in a professional manner.
- Consistently deliver on time, keep the client updated on delivery schedules, and inform them of any changes.
- Understand that the customer is always right, and without them, there is no income.
- You only employ people who understand and live the client service philosophy.
- Always maintain a direct line of contact with your clients. If possible, 24/7.
- Keep all social media up-to-date and current.
- Document ALL contacts within a client's business.

Simon finished writing his list and closed his notebook.

"Please do not lose or stop living that list." Isaac said.

Simon said he would and moved his notepad to his seat as the waitress arrived with his order.

"Excuse me, sir," she said, placing the cups and pot of tea on the table. "Firstly, I must apologise for not including sugar in your coffee as requested yesterday. Additionally, I apologise for directing you to retrieve the sugar yourself when I should have done it for you. Finally, I would like to offer these drinks on the house as a gesture of sincerity for my mistake."

Simon sat feeling very guilty for the snide comment he had made to Isaac on his way to order. Isaac just sat with the usual smile, obviously knowing more was about to unfold.

Simon moved his coffee mug further onto the table and away from the edge, then looked up at the waitress. She was wearing black pants and a white blouse with the business name embroidered on the upper left. She seemed concerned about the situation.

"Apology accepted. Also, you are a business and need income, so please inform the boss that I will cover the cost of our order."

Clearly now even more embarrassed, the waitress held the tray up a little higher to cover her red face. "I am the boss," she said in a soft voice.

Simon was taken aback and looked toward Isaac for some support.

Isaac just sat, his expression totally unchanged, like a patron in a theatre watching a well-rehearsed play unfold in front of them.

Evidently not getting any support from Isaac, Simon stood and faced her.

"Oh, wow," he started, not sure what to say. Gathering his thoughts, he continued. "Congratulations, how long have you had the business?"

Lowering the serving tray to her chest, and her face colour returning to some normality, she replied, "I purchased it from an elderly couple about six months ago.

I have been making changes when I can afford them, but I know not to rush. I used to work in retail; however, I always dreamed of having my own business. After a bit of encouragement from a friend I met one day, I took the leap, and here I am. I am working on a plan and hope to be expanding to include restaurant down the track. Just got to follow the plan."

"Well, I wish you luck, and be assured, should I have any need for meetings with my clients, I will be sure to come here," Simon said, then added, "I am also just starting up a new venture. My friend here is helping me." Simon turned and pointed across to Isaac.

The waitress, however, kept her focus on Simon, not appearing at all interested in the small old Asian man on the couch.

"Well, congratulations to you as well," she said, lowering the tray to her left side, she held out he hand. "My name is Jenny."

Simon, taking her hand, replied. "Simon. Again, good luck. Best get back to the coffee before it gets too cold and thank you for your kind offer; however, I will be up shortly to pay you." putting emphasis on the, "I will."

Jenny turned and headed back to her station behind the counter.

Isaac continued to sit and smile. "Lesson," he said without the slightest change in the expression.

Simon figured it was not rhetorical. "Umm, point one on my list: honesty," he replied.

"Correct. And for number 13 on your list, I will give you this as a freebie: respect. What you said to me as you left for the counter may have appeared to be incorrect. Respect is maybe one of the most important attributes needed in any business, and it must be earned. It is never given. Do you recall "My colleague, who owns the transport business?"

Simon nodded. Isaac continued, "He was once on a train when an elderly lady boarded. All the carriages seats were full. He stood up and said loudly enough for her and the nearby passengers to hear, 'Please have my seat.'

"She responded, 'Thank you for your kind gesture, but I am only going to the next station.' My colleague smiled politely and turned to sit back down; however, a young, well-dressed man moved quickly across and sat in the seat. The young man merely smirked at my colleague and then, proceeded to look to his phone."

"Later that day the PA called her boss and told him the candidate from their Yorkshire office, for the new sales manager position, had arrived," Isaac paused, then said, "And yes, he was on time."

A smile of understanding crossed Simon's face.

Isaac continued, "My colleague approached the gentleman and asked, 'Mister Thompson?' while extending his hand. The man leaned forward in his seat to retrieve his briefcase and stood up, and replied 'Yes,' but missed the handshake as it was withdrawn and then pulled his own hand back."

"My colleague stood for some rather uncomfortable seconds while he contemplated his next move. 'Please, Mister… uh, what's your name again?' he asked, pointing down the hall."

"'Thompson, Peter Thompson,' the candidate replied'".

"They headed down to the office, where my colleague walked behind his desk and sat. The man entered the office and reached for a seat in one of the chairs on the opposite side of the desk. 'No', my colleague said, shaking his head, then added, 'what's your name again. Oh, doesn't matter. You can stand over there in the corner.'"

Isaac paused and smiled as he understood the look of astonishment on Simon's face.

"Bit rude… your colleague," Simon said, in the pause.

"One would assume so, but again incorrect," Isaac replied, "Let me continue."

"The candidate looked around the room, more as a reaction to see if there were other people who might be watching this weird request. Then he looked over to the nearest corner, which was to the left of the door he had just come through and pointed. 'This corner?' My colleague just nodded, then began typing."

"The man went to the corner and turned back to the desk. He started to say something, but my colleague held up his hand and continued typing. After a few minutes passed the printer behind the desk spun up. Moments later, a sheet of paper came out. My colleague took it and folded it. He then signalled for the man to come from the corner and stand at the desk."

"'Mister Thompson, I am sure you are a capable salesman and would maybe make an OK sales manager; however, your attitude towards the art of politeness and particularly respect needs a lot of work. A lot,' he emphasised."

Isaac continued. "'I have here a copy of the email I just sent to your boss. It outlines your actions this morning on a train when I stood to allow an elderly lady to sit and you, rudely,' then he added, 'very rudely, took the seat even before the lady had finished her reply.'"

Isaac stopped his story.

Simon looked at Isaac. "So, what did the note say, and what happened to the man?"

"Both are totally wrong questions," Isaac replied. "You need to give me an answer at your new office tomorrow as to both the lesson from my story and also why the other two questions are irrelevant?"

"But how will I explain it to Judy, um… my wife, about you?"

"Not a problem, I will be there after she has gone to work."

Chapter Fourteen

It had been a long night for Simon. When he arrived home after his meeting with Isaac he found over thirty emails, most from people he had sent emails to letting them know of his new venture. Some just wished him well. He replied to them and added them to his CRM. It had been the backbone of his time at the old company and would remain so in his new company.

He ensured that he entered essential details, such as a spouse's name, children's names, and other small details that would assist him, and later, a customer service team, in making their job easier. Promises and important conversation pieces were also part of the ritual. This included keeping notes in the book of gold, as he called it, his notebook. In it was the daily To-Do List, with any items from the previous day that were not completed moved to the new day's list.

Crossing off items from his To-Do List always gave him great satisfaction. The last thing to be completed today was the physical filing of the invoices. He always printed a copy of an invoice and wrote any important information on it. Whether it was, delivery being held up, a phone call, a time and date, that may for some obscure reason be needed in the future.

He recalled one such instance from his previous job, when the boss called him into his office because a client had complained that the computer he had purchased two years earlier did not have the correct amount of memory and was now useless.

Simon had gone to the folder for that period and found the order and invoice stapled together. On the order, he had written the time and date of a call he had made to the client, and the note read 'suggested the memory remain as spec. The customer refused, as he wanted the cheapest computer possible.'

This fact, particularly the time and date of the phone call, saved the company a lot of money. Simon had called the client and reminded him of the call, then offered a memory upgrade with free installation. The customer was happy, as was the boss, as the margin on the memory covered not only its cost but the installation and a reasonable profit to boot.

Filing finished, Simon headed into the kitchen to help Judy.

"How was your day?" he asked as he headed over to

the oven to check on the roast. He knew it was chicken, as he had spent the past hour savouring the smells emanating from this favoured room of their modest home.

"Not too bad," Judy replied, "Fixed the problem with the software and think I have found who was taking the spare parts out of inventory. So, the rest of the week will be sorting that out. Do you mind making the gravy?" she asked, handing him a skillet. Simon enjoyed this tiny portion of the preparation. "So, how was your meeting with Mr Isaac?"

Simon hesitated as he didn't like talking about Isaac. He still was not sure if he was real. He thought about how stupid this was and some of the things he seemed to know.

He added the ingredients to the skillet and placed it on the stove.

"It went well. He wants me to have some answers for him tomorrow when he comes here." He bit his tongue as soon as he had said the words.

"Oh, what time?" Judy asked excitedly. She had often asked if she would ever meet this mysterious man.

"He's not coming till after ten," Simon replied, even though they had never mentioned an actual time, just that it would be after Judy had gone to work. Simon just assumed Isaac would know Judy left at nine thirty. "How," he said out loud.

"How what?" Judy asked, stirring the gravy as she passed the stove.

"Nothing," Simon replied. "He has asked me to have an answer for the meeting."

Simon spent the remainder of the meal preparation telling Judy the story of the man on the train.

They sat at the dining table and started the meal. Judy settled and was about to start her meal,

"So clearly, he was rude, and my guess is that the guy didn't get the job, and most likely the email his boss got would mean he lost his job." she said as the first bite of dinner headed up to her mouth.

"That is if the note was to tell him what had transpired on his way to the head office." Simon replied, then continued, "and yes, the story is about the rudeness of the man, but that is way too easy an answer to this question."

Dinner over, Judy placed her cutlery and her plate on the sink. "So not rudeness, punctuality or attire. This guy clearly couldn't recall the boss fellow, but the boss recalled this guy. So what? Got me stumped," she said.

Simon, standing at the sink finishing the chore he hated the most, washing-up, then flicked the sponge at Judy. "I know exactly what to say. Thank you," he said, wiping the water off Judy's nose with the tea towel, before kissing her on the forehead. She just shook her head and headed to the lounge.

. . .

Chapter Fifteen

Breakfast done, Simon grabbed his phone off the charger and headed into the office. It was seven a.m. when he pulled up a chair and switched on the computer. As it booted up, he opened his phone. The first "How the hell does he do it," for the day was expressed.

The text read:

Good morning, Simon,

I figured last night that we may need to meet, so how does 12:30 pm at the coffee shop sound?

Great, See you then.

Isaac.

Simon knew that midday traffic was bad, so he left, giving himself plenty of time to account for potential delays. He arrived and parked, still with ten minutes up his sleeve. He decided to head to the coffee shop and find a spare table. He was sure it would be busy with the lunch crowd.

Arriving at the door, he noted that his fear was well-founded. The place was packed. There was a queue at the counter; however, looking to his right, Simon noted the couch by the window was empty. He looked towards the line and saw Jenny working at the coffee machine, and another lady taking orders. Out the back, he heard what he assumed was a cook and possibly a helper. Jenny looked up over the top of the mugs sitting atop the silver hissing coffee machine. She pointed to the lounge and indicated by lifting her index finger and mouthing the words "be a minute."

Simon took up his position, and as promised, Jenny turned up sixty seconds later.

"Hi Simon, you here by yourself or waiting on a client?"

After looking around, Simon replied. "Wow, the place is packed, and I guess Isaac, my friend from the other day, must have phoned and booked this spot?"

Jenny screwed up her face and shook her head, not understanding. "No, no one named Isaac phoned. It just seemed no one wanted to sit near the window."

Simon just smiled. He didn't even need to think of the usual words that went with his now-shaking head. He was curious, "So the friend who you said had helped you. Does he have a name?"

"You know, I don't recall. He was there to help, but I don't recall a name or even what he looked like…"

Jenny never finished her answer as Isaac had arrived at the door. She turned and looked at him. "Good afternoon, sir, would you like a table?"

"No thanks, I am meeting Simon here. Would it be possible to get him his regular, and I would love a pot of tea?"

"Sure," she replied and turned to Simon. "Talk later,", she said, turning back to the counter.

As Isaac sat, he looked at Simon. "The answer to your thought about her is yes, now you need to give me an answer to your question."

Simon was about to ask another question about Jenny, but for some reason, he forgot it and returned to the questioning from Isaac. Not bothering to even entertain the thought of a "how" question, he just looked blankly at the smiling Isaac. However, he needed an answer to his "Fast Growing" question.

Isaac shifted in his seat. "Let me help a little by finishing up our sporting goods story."

Simon then took up his trusty notebook and yet another new pen, setting them on the table, and proudly smiled, both inwardly and outwardly.

Isaac shuffled a little in his seat and began, "Our friend pleased his new client by delivering all the tennis rackets on time as promised. His business, like yours, was growing, and he pondered his next move. He knew from business books, that he had read, using software, such as an accounting package or a CRM package, instead of hiring a new employee, could boost productivity at a lower long-term cost."

Isaac then added, looking down at the notebook and pen being gathered up by Simon, "Software is a onetime cost, usually with a small annual maintenance expense, whereas an employee incurs yearly ongoing costs."

Isaac then continued the story. "His challenge was managing his time effectively and keeping a control on the growth of the business. He realised that 80% of his day was spent attending to clients who were generating only 20% of his revenue. Moreover, 80% of orders originated from 20% of customers.

"Consequently, he made the difficult decision to inform underperforming clients that it might be in their best interest to seek another supplier. In some cases, he discreetly provided his most capable competitor with the names of these non-performing clients. He then focused on dedicating 80% of his time to the top-performing 20% of customers. Additionally, he allocated 10% of his time to acquiring new clients and the remaining 10% to addressing the needs of the lower-performing 80%."

"According to most business studies, acquiring a new client is 5 to 25 times more expensive than retaining an existing one, provided his client is in the high preforming 20th percentile."

"He always used the, next door and across the street rule, for any new client,". Isaac explained "This, referred to the painter, builder or repairman, who would drop next door and across the road to either speak with the neighbour about their neighbour, who was happy to be using his or her services. If the neighbour were not home, then they would leave a card. In the case of our guy," he explained, "he would request from the happy new client the name or a contact person or a company that could use the man's sporting goods business."

"Our friend applied all these new rules to his business and to this day is enjoying sustainable growth."

Simon had finished and Jenny had delivered the coffee and tea during the telling of the story. He finally looked up at Simon. "So, answer to your question?"

As usual, Simon had not even asked but gathered his thoughts.

"In the story, you used the words sustainable growth. So, my answer is that I look at my customer base and apply the rules our friend applied to his business. I need an assistant to do all the office stuff so I can better spend the 80% of my time with my good customers. I think I know the best person for this job."

Isaac jumped in. "That person you are considering would be good however you are breaking one of your rules," he said, then held up his hand just as Simon was about to speak. Isaac smiled as Jenny approached the table.

"Can I get you guys anything else?" she asked gathering up the empty vessels.

Simon looked at Isaac for an answer. Isaac sat as he had been since he had lowered his hand, so no answer was obviously forthcoming.

Simon turned to Jenny and was about to say "no" when he noticed the café had emptied and three other people were cleaning up and thanking the patrons heading out the door.

"So, Jenny, do you mind if I ask you a question?" Simon asked.

"Sure!"

"As you know, I have started a business of my own and I need a trusted and hard-working person to help me with my clerical and office stuff. So, my question is how did you choose your first employee?"

Jenny didn't respond but looked at a nearby lady carrying a tray of empty glasses and plates.

"Hey Susanne, could you get my notebook from the back when you have a moment?" she called out, then sat next to Isaac, in a manner that indicated she was not interested in the person next to her.

Simon looked at Isaac, who smiled in a way Simon had never seen before. Simon then forgot why he looked at him and returned his attention to Jenny.

She settled, then started her answer, "I was in exactly the same predicament about five months ago. After several advertisements, I broke one of my rules. I talked to my sister, and she agreed to help me till I found someone who was not a friend or family. As I said, that was five months ago, and after several hiccups, here we are still loving sisters and about to purchase the place next door and expand into a restaurant." As she finished her answer, Susanne arrived, notebook in hand. "Simon, meet Susanne, the first and now full-time employee for the soon-to-open TCM restaurant."

"Let me guess," Simon said excitedly, "Tea, Coffee &… Meals?"

"Spot on," she replied, then added, "So family is OK on a trial basis to briefly fill a spot that will clearly be filled later. That way, everyone is clear of the intended outcome."

She continued as she opened her notebook, "I have all my rules written here in the back."

Simon just smiled and turned to where Isaac had sat. There was no one there, so he turned back to Jenny.

They continued to compare notes and updated each other's lists. They finished after three p.m. Simon was not sure why he had come to the café but was so glad he had.

He returned home and was in the process of putting an ad together for an office assistant when Judy came through the door in tears. Simon ran to her.

"What happened?

"They retrenched me."

Chapter Sixteen

It was the day before Simon's daughter's first birthday. He was returning from a meeting in London with the soon-to-be fourth member of his board, that so far, consisted of him, Judy, and Sam, who had quit the same day Judy was retrenched. Simon called her the following day and offered her the job of office manager at twice her previous salary as a PA. Now he had discovered that he needed a third-party board member to be able to look inward at the company's activities and provide advice when needed.

On the way to the train station, he had stopped to purchase a gift for Julia, his beautiful newborn daughter. Securely tucked under his arm was a gold and black striped stuffed toy tiger, wrapped in pink paper, with a birthday card attached. As he boarded, he wondered what the new name for this black and gold fluffy toy would be.

Once on the train, he noted all seats were taken except for one beside a casually dressed man, who appeared slumped in the window seat. He decided not to sit there. Not sure why he left it empty. Moments later, an elderly Asian man wearing an old ill-fitting suit, entered the carriage and made his way to the empty seat.

"Do you mind?" he asked, pointing to the seat.

The man seated by the window just nodded and returned his gaze to the inky blackness of the train tunnel. The frail man sat. Then, once settled, pulled out a deck of cards.

Simon had no urge to take any further interest in the pair.

'Maybe she will call this cute toy Tigger,' he thought.

The 12 Commandments

HOW TO BE BETTER THAN YOUR COMPETITOR.

- Honesty.
- Respect. (Has to be earned)
- Punctuality
- Discipline
- Understanding communication. This includes getting back to clients every time you say or communicate you will. You will also do so either at or before a specified time no matter if you have an answer or not.
- Dress and always appear and behave in a professional manner.
- Always deliver the goods on time and keep the client informed of delivery dates and times and advise them of any changes.
- Understand that the customer is always right, and without them there is no income.
- You only employ people who understand and live client service.
- Always have an avenue of direct contact with your clients. If possible 24x7.
- Keep all social media up-to-date and current.
- Document ALL contacts within a client's business.

Rules

- You have one mouth and two ears to be used in that ratio.
- Learn to and always practice being very comfortable around silence.
- When working from home, retain your usual business attire and routines as you would in your outside workplace.
- Talking negatively about your competitor, former employers, and ex-colleagues is always a fatal mistake.
- Always keep your desk tidy, remove all documents at the end of the day, and ensure that if visitors are present in the office, sensitive documents are not on desks.
- Always keep a diary and a notebook. They are your best friend.
- Anyone is a potential client or your future boss.
- Use software whenever possible, as people are a much higher ongoing cost.
- 80- 20 rule
- Acquiring a new client is 5 to 25 times more expensive than retaining an existing good one.

- Ten percent of all you earn is yours to keep.[1]
- Find a good and trusted accountant. Paying more not less applies "You get what you pay for"
- Stay with what you know and understand, and don't take on something someone has told you will be great for your business if you don't know anything about it.
- Friends or family often never make good business partners or employees.
- Set up a simple address policy. Do not allow personal email addresses onto company software. Include an info@ address that, must be checked at least once a day.
- Have a fully documented and implemented Policies and Procedures manual, no matter how small or large the business.
- A sale is not a sale till the funds (nett profit) are cleared and, in the bank.
- Apply the next door and across the street rule.
- Always put aside time to rest and remain fit.

Your Rules

- ....

---

1. Quote from the book by George S. Calson (2008) *The Richest Man in Babylon.* Signet. (Original work published 1926)

THANK YOU FOR READING

I sincerely hope you found inspiration and enjoyment in The Mysterious Mr Isaac.

As an author, I truly value feedback from readers – it helps my work grow and reach others who might benefit from it too.

If you enjoyed the story, I'd be incredibly grateful if you could share your thoughts by leaving an honest review on Amazon, or even posting on social media using the tags @RickBrownAuthor.

Your support makes a real difference.

If you'd like to get in touch directly, or join my Advanced Readers List, feel free to email me at rickb@rickbrownauthor.com.au. I personally reply to every message and always enjoy hearing your reflections on the book.

Warmest wishes,
Rick Brown

About the Author

After a successful career in the corporate world, Rick found solace and inspiration in the tranquil beauty of the Whitsundays. Surrounded by pristine beaches and azure waters, he rekindled his lifelong passion for storytelling. Rick's stories weave together threads of real-life experiences and the boundless realm of imagination, capturing the essence and resilience of the human spirit. Rick is dedicated to creating narratives that not only entertain but also deeply resonate with readers, inviting them to explore the profound beauty and complexity of life.

Please visit my website RickBrownAuthor.com.au